My book of
SPECIAL TIMES
in church

Anne Faulkner is Parish Development Adviser for Buckingham within the diocese of Oxford, and a Reader in the Church of England. She is author of Barnabas' popular seasonal books for children, *The Advent Alphabet* and *The Easter Alphabet*, and *My book of Special Times of year* in the *Church and Me* range.

To Sue, Hilary and Caroline,
who have taught me so much over the
years and who are such fun to be with.

Church and me
A welcome book for children

My book of
SPECIAL TIMES
in church

ANNE FAULKNER

Text copyright © Anne Faulkner 1999
The author asserts the moral right
to be identified as the author of this work

Published by
The Bible Reading Fellowship
Peter's Way, Sandy Lane West
Oxford OX4 5HG
ISBN 1 84101 067 7

First published 1999
1 3 5 7 9 10 8 6 4 2 0
All rights reserved

Acknowledgments

Unless otherwise stated, scripture quotations are taken from the
Good News Bible published by The Bible Societies/HarperCollins
Publishers Ltd, UK © American Bible Society 1966, 1971,
1976, 1992, used with permission.

A catalogue record for this book is available from the
British Library

Printed and bound in Great Britain
by Caledonian Book Manufacturing International, Glasgow

INTRODUCTION

Families like to share all kinds of times. They meet together for happy times like birthdays, or weddings. They also meet at sad times like when someone is ill or when someone has died. Sometimes families meet for a meal, or they might share a day out or a holiday together.

The church family meets together too. There are many kinds of different times when we can meet in church. Some of the times are happy, like a baptism, and some are sad, like a funeral. Some of these special times happen often, like Holy Communion or a Family Service. Some of them only happen once a year, like a Crib Service or a Pets' Service. Whenever they happen, God wants all his family in the church to share them together.

Look inside this book and find out more about God's special times in church. There are things for you to read about. There are things for you to look for in your own church. And there are things for you to do.

Do have fun as you use this book.

HOLY COMMUNION—
JESUS' PARTY

Things to see in church

a cup called a chalice

special clothes worn by the minister

a cup with a lid, called a ciborium

a plate called a paten

bread and wine

candles lit on the altar

Colour in the pictures of the things you have seen.

About Holy Communion

This is a special time when people gather together in church to share bread and wine.

It is Jesus' special party that he invites us to. It is a time for everyone to be happy. Because it is Jesus' party, some churches use a cup and a plate made of very beautiful silver or gold.

Sometimes there are crowds of people there, with singing and musicians, and the service takes quite a long time. At other times there are very few people there. Then the service is quiet and only takes a little while.

A Bible verse for Holy Communion

While they were eating, Jesus took a piece of bread, gave a prayer of thanks, broke it and gave it to his disciples... Then he took the cup, gave thanks to God, and gave it to them.

Matthew 26:26–27

What do you like best about parties?

I really enjoy the special food like tiny sausages, cheese and pineapple on sticks, and the birthday cake. Good food makes for a good party.

Holy Communion is Jesus' party. The special food at this party is bread and wine. This is because Jesus told us that when we eat bread and wine together, just like he did with his friends, he would always be with us.

> Thank you, Jesus, for giving us Holy Communion. Thank you for bread and wine that help us to know how much you love us. Amen

Something to do for Holy Communion

Colour these pictures of:

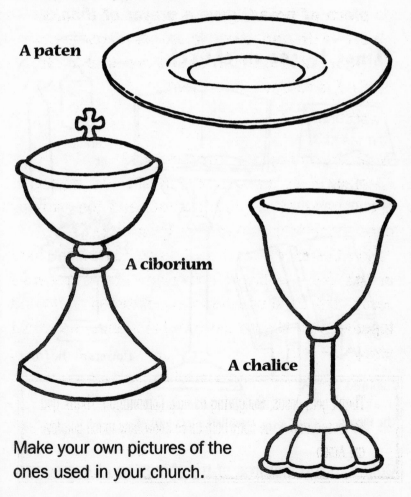

A paten

A ciborium

A chalice

Make your own pictures of the
ones used in your church.

MORNING AND EVENING PRAYER

Things to see in church

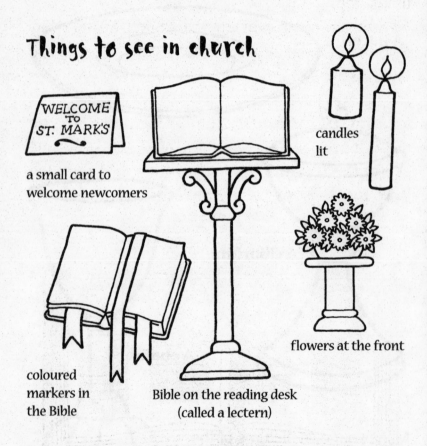

WELCOME TO ST. MARK'S

a small card to welcome newcomers

candles lit

coloured markers in the Bible

Bible on the reading desk (called a lectern)

flowers at the front

Colour in the pictures of the things you have seen.

About Morning and Evening Prayer

As well as special times in our lives, we have ordinary times, too.

There are some ordinary things that we do every day. One of these is to say 'good morning' and 'good night' to people.

Morning and Evening Prayer are times in church for us to say 'good morning' to God and to say 'good night' to him at the end of the day. They are gentle services with or without singing and music, and the Bible is always read aloud for all to hear.

A Bible verse for Morning and Evening Prayer

You created the day and the night; you set the sun and moon in their places.

Psalm 74:16

Some people get up very early in the morning. If you ever do that, you will know how quiet it is before everyone starts being busy.

When it gets dark and everyone goes indoors, it can be a time of quiet too. Even the birds go to bed before it gets dark and so they are quiet.

Each day is a gift from God. In church we sometimes begin and end the day by saying 'good morning' and 'good night' to God in Morning and Evening Prayer.

Father God, you give us mornings and evenings. Help us to remember to say 'good morning' and 'good night' to you each day. Amen

Something to do for Morning and Evening Prayer

Draw a big sun and a big moon. Then draw or write round them all the things that you like about the early morning and about the night.

BAPTISM—WELCOME TO GOD'S FAMILY

Things to see in church

font, a basin or a pool

a shell

the big Easter candle (Paschal Candle)

small candle for person being baptized

a big jug

water

things that are white

Colour in the pictures of the things you have seen.

About baptism

All animals, plants and people need water to stay alive.

At a baptism, water is used as a sign of new life for the person being baptized. Promises are made by the godparents and parents, or by the adult being baptized.

A person who has been baptized belongs to God in a special way and he or she is welcomed as a new member of God's family, which is the church.

Sometimes a baby is baptized. Sometimes it is an adult or an older child who is baptized. The water is poured over the person's head and a small shell is used to scoop up the water. In some churches there is a pool, a bit like a small swimming pool, and the person goes right into the water.

A lighted candle is often given to those who are newly baptized, to take home to remind them that Jesus is the light of the world, and they belong to Jesus.

A Bible verse for baptism

Many of them believed his message and were baptized.

Acts 2:41

Who is in your family? In most families we all try to help each other because we love each other. Children can help grown-ups, and older people can help children. What do you help with?

When we are baptized, we are all members of God's family. This family is a big one but we still all try to help each other. When a new member is welcomed at baptism, everyone is very pleased.

Those people who are baptized meet together in church to worship God and to be his family.

> Dear God, we thank you for water, which gives life to your world. We ask you to bless all those who are newly baptized and we thank you for all those members of your big family, the church. Amen

Something to do for baptism

Draw or collect pictures of different ways in which we use water in our lives. Here are some to get you started.

THANKSGIVING FOR THE BIRTH OF A BABY

Things to see in church

The church will look very much as usual. There are no special things to look for, but see if you can find these:

the big
Easter candle
(Paschal
Candle)

candles

flowers

Colour in the pictures of the things you have seen.

About thanksgiving for the birth of a baby

When a new baby is born, everyone gets very excited. People send cards and presents. Friends and family try to see the baby as soon as they can.

People want to know what the baby will be called and they try to guess who the baby looks like.

A new baby is a gift from God. Sometimes parents want to say 'thank you' to God for this gift. They meet in church with their family and tell God how pleased they are and how grateful they are to him that the baby has arrived safely.

A Bible verse for thanksgiving for the birth of a baby

Jesus took the children in his arms, placed his hands on each of them, and blessed them.

Mark 10:16

When a baby is born, we all want to hold it in our arms and cuddle it. We can hardly believe that we were once that small and helpless.

One day when Jesus was with his friends, he told everyone how important children are. He made sure that his friends knew that children are very special.

God is pleased when parents bring a baby to church for a blessing and to say 'thank you' for such a precious present.

Dear Jesus, thank you for all the love you show to children everywhere. Help them all to know how much you love them. Amen

Something to do for thanking God for a new baby

Make a strip of children holding hands.

Fold a piece of paper measuring 35cm x 12cm as shown. Draw a figure on the front. Cut out, making sure the folded edges are left intact.

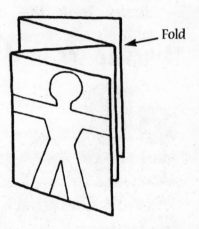

Fold

Colour the figures to look like your friends and write their names on each figure.

MARRIAGE—THANK YOU FOR SPECIAL LOVE

Things to see in church

people wearing
their best
clothes

flowers
in vases

balloons, ribbons and
other decorations

the bride and bridesmaids
wearing long dresses

flowers being carried as bouquets
and worn as buttonholes

things that are white

Colour in the pictures of the things you have seen.

About marriage

Two people get married in church because they want God to be part of their future life together.

They promise to love one another and they are given God's blessing.

They often give each other a ring as a sign of their love.

A wedding is a very happy time and people getting married like to make the church look special, with decorations of all kinds. It is usual for the most important people, the bride, the bridegroom and their close family and friends, to have new clothes especially for the day.

A Bible verse for marriage

My commandment is this: love one another, just as I love you.

John 15:12

We all need people to love us, whatever age we are. When two people get married, they love each other so much that they want to be together and to share everything that they have.

Jesus knows that this is not always easy, so he wants to bless their love to help them to go on loving each other.

Jesus loves us all and he wants us to love each other.

Loving Jesus, we thank you for your love to us all. Help us to love others too, especially when we feel grumpy or cross. Amen

---

Something to do for marriage

Decorate these two hearts with flowers or in some other way.

CONFIRMATION—YOU ARE GROWN UP NOW

Things to see in church

pictures of doves

the bishop

pictures of flames of fire

things that are white

Colour in the pictures of the things you have seen.

About confirmation

Can you do up your own shoes? Can you feed yourself using a knife and fork? Can you clean your own teeth?

When you were very small, you could not do very much for yourself, but as you have grown older you have been able to do more and more.

When babies are baptized, they are welcomed into God's family, but it is the parents who make promises for them. It is the parents who have to do everything for them. Without help from parents, a baby could not go to church or know about God's love.

Confirmation is about growing up and about making the promises for yourself.

At a confirmation, the bishop confirms people by putting his hands on their heads and asking for the Holy Spirit of God to fill their lives.

A Bible verse for confirmation

Jesus said to them, 'Come with me, and I will teach you how to catch people.'
Mark 1:17

When you learn to do things for yourself, it is grown-ups or older sisters and brothers who help you. You learn all kinds of things from others.

When we are confirmed, we promise to be a friend of Jesus and to learn more and more about him. God knows that this is not easy, so he sends his Holy Spirit to help us.

It is not easy for us to imagine the Holy Spirit of God, so pictures of fire and wind, or the sign of a dove, are used to help us.

Father God, we ask you to help us to grow up to love you more and more and to be one of your friends. Amen

Something to do for confirmation

Copy two doves and two lots of flames on to thin card, colour them and cut them out round the outside circles.

Draw and colour your own doves and flames on the blank side of the card. Make a small hole in the top of each circle. Thread through pieces of string or wool that are different lengths. Tie the other end of the string or wool to the bar of a wire coathanger. Hang the mobile up by the hook of the coathanger.

A FUNERAL—JESUS, WE ARE SAD

Things to see in church

special flowers made up into wreaths

things that are purple

people being sad and crying

people in dark clothes

the coffin on a stand

Colour in the pictures of the things you have seen.

About funerals

When someone we love dies, we feel sad and do not feel like laughing and having fun.

The person who has died has gone to be with Jesus, so we are happy for them, especially if they have been ill or if they were very old. But we are sad that we cannot see them any more.

A funeral is a service to say 'goodbye' to the person we love and to thank God for all that we can remember about them.

Family and friends often give special flowers. These are put on or near the coffin, which is a box specially made to carry the person who has died.

A Bible verse for a funeral

'Do not be worried and upset,' Jesus told his friends. 'Believe in God and believe also in me. There are many rooms in my Father's house and I am going to prepare a place for you.'

John 14:1–2

When we are sad, there are people in our lives who try to cheer us up.

When we are sad because someone we love has died, Jesus tries to cheer us up. The words of this Bible passage remind us that the person who has died has gone to be with Jesus. When our turn comes to die and we are with Jesus, we will see the person we love once more.

Thank you for promising us that you will always be with us when we are sad. We thank you that one day we will see again those people we love who have died. Amen

Something to do for a funeral

Design a card that you could give to someone who is sad because someone they love has died.

Thinking of You

A CRIB SERVICE—
HAPPY BIRTHDAY, JESUS

Things to see in church

extra candles

the crib, with the figures of
Mary and Joseph in the stable,
perhaps with shepherds and angels

Christmas decorations

the figure of
baby Jesus
(which may or
may not be in
the crib)

Colour in the pictures of the things you have seen.

About crib services

Christmas is a very exciting time. In the middle of all the thinking about presents, food, and parties, we must remember that it is Jesus' birthday.

Crib services are usually held on Christmas Eve and they help us to think about baby Jesus. Sometimes they are held with everyone standing round the crib. Sometimes the figures are carried to the crib in the service.

Sometimes people are dressed up and a 'real' crib is made.

A Bible verse for a crib service

So the shepherds hurried off and found Mary and Joseph and saw the baby lying in the manger.

Luke 2:16

Most children like to play with models. Perhaps you have a toy farm, a doll's house, a castle or a garage to play with. You might have a small crib at home so that you can play with the figures of Mary, Joseph and baby Jesus.

In church we have a crib to remind us of the Christmas story. Sometimes the figures are quite heavy and they cost a lot of money, so we can't play with them. But a crib service helps us to look closely at the crib and to hear the Christmas story again.

Thank you, Father God, for giving us Jesus, who came as a tiny baby. Help us to remember that Christmas is his birthday. Amen

Something to do for a crib service

Make your own crib out of playdough. Here is a recipe for dough if you need it. Ask a grown-up to help you.

You will need:
two cups of plain flour,
one cup of salt,
two cups of water,
two teaspoons of cream
of tartar,
two tablespoons of
cooking oil, and
food colourings.

1. Put all ingredients into a pan and cook for about three minutes.
2. Vary the colour of your dough by adding a drop of food colouring.
3. When cooked, remove from the pan and knead into a ball. (Sprinkle a little flour on to the surface where the dough is to be used.)

4. The dough will last for about a week if stored in a sealed plastic container when not in use.

A PRAM SERVICE—GOD LOVES LITTLE CHILDREN

Things to see in church

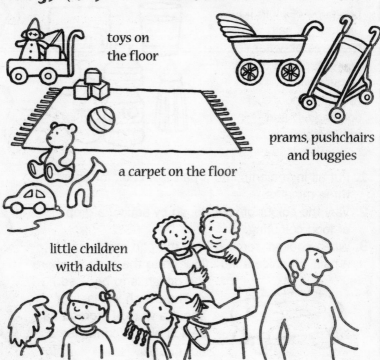

toys on the floor

prams, pushchairs and buggies

a carpet on the floor

little children with adults

Colour in the pictures of the things you have seen.

About pram services

Pram services are usually held on weekdays. They are for adults and little children together. Because the children are very small, they need toys to play with.

They sing very simple songs and the service is short. It is often followed by drinks of squash and biscuits.

A Bible verse for a pram service

Jesus said, 'Whoever welcomes in my name one of these children, welcomes me.'

Mark 9:37

What are the names of your friends? Little children do not go to school and they cannot go out to play, so they need to have special places to meet their friends.

Pram services give them a chance to meet and to learn more about Jesus. God loves children to play and to be happy together, as they are very special to him.

Thank you, Lord Jesus, that little children are so important to you. Help us always to be kind to them when we play with them. Amen

Something to do for a pram service

Here is a picture of a pram service. How many toys can you find in the picture?

A TOY SERVICE—GIVING IS GOOD

Things to see in church

toys of all kinds

parcels and boxes

a Christmas tree

large baskets or boxes to collect toys

Colour in the pictures of the things you have seen.

About toy services

We all like to get presents.

Toy services give us a chance to give presents to others. They are often held before Christmas. Toys are brought to church and collected up. After the service, they are taken to children who do not get many toys to play with.

A Bible verse for a toy service

'Love your neighbour as you love yourself.'
Matthew 22:39

We all get very excited when we think we might get a present on our birthday, when a special relative comes, or at Christmas. Can you think of any presents that you have had?

Jesus knows that we all like getting presents. But he also knows that it is lovely for us to give presents to others, too.

> Help us, loving God, to think of others and not just about ourselves. Help us to enjoy giving to other people. Amen

Something to do for a toy service

Which toys do you think are in these parcels?
Draw pictures of toys around the parcels.

A PETS' SERVICE

Things to see in church

larger pets, like horses,
which are rather big
to go in church

the furniture moved
out of the way

lots of people with their pets
outside the church building
or in a field near the church

lots of
newspaper on
the floor

smaller pets
in cages

Colour in the pictures of the things you have seen.

About pets' services

We love the animals we keep as pets. They are part of our family life.

Some churches have special services for pets. At these we can thank God for all the love and happiness our pets give us. They become part of our church family, too.

A Bible verse for a pets' service

Lord, you have made so many things! The earth is filled with your creatures.

Psalm 104:24

Some of us have small pets, like mice and goldfish. Some of us have pets that live indoors, like cats and dogs. Some of us have big pets that live outside, like horses and goats. Some of us cannot have pets, but we enjoy sharing other people's.

All our pets matter to God and are part of the world that he made to praise him.

Dear God, thank you for our pets that you made for us to enjoy. Please help us to be kind to all animals. Amen

---

Something to do for a pets' service

Can you guess which pets these are? Tick the ones you like the best.

CHRISTINGLE—LIGHT IN THE DARKNESS

Things to see in church

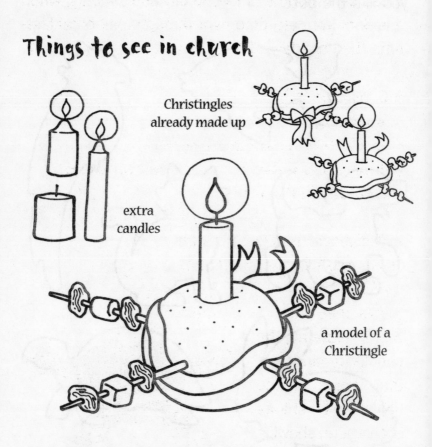

Christingles already made up

extra candles

a model of a Christingle

Colour in the pictures of the things you have seen.

About a Christingle service

Christingle services are services of light held during those dark months of December and January, when it is dark from tea-time right through until breakfast-time the next day.

A Christingle is made of:
- **an orange**
- **a red ribbon round the orange**
- **four sticks with sweets or fruit on them**
- **a candle in the top**

A Christingle reminds us that Jesus died for all the world and that God gives us the good things that grow all over the world. Above all, the candle reminds us that Jesus is the light that shines everywhere, showing his love for us all.

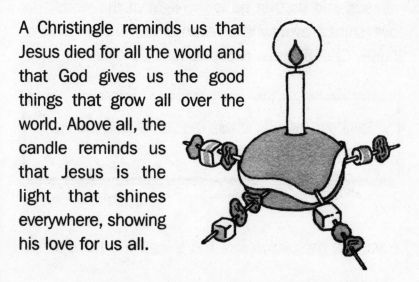

A Bible verse for Christingle

'I am the light of the world,' Jesus said. 'Whoever follows me will have the light of life and will never walk in darkness.'

John 8:12

Some nights, the light of the moon shines very brightly through my bedroom window. Sometimes it is so bright that it wakes me up, but it is lovely to see it. We could not manage life at all without the light of the moon and the sun.

Jesus told us that he is the light of the world. His love shines everywhere, even when we are sad or lonely. Christingle services remind us of this.

Thank you, Jesus, for all your love, and for being there for us at all times in our lives. Amen

Something to do for Christingle

Colour this Christingle or ask a grown-up to help you make one of your own.

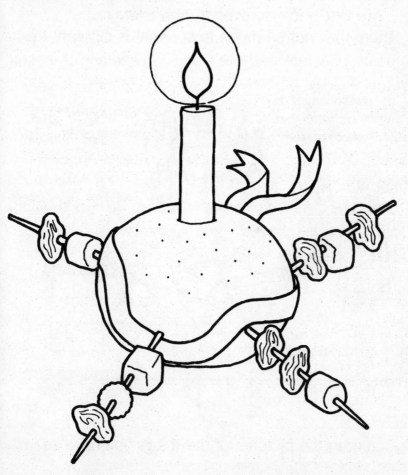

A FAMILY SERVICE

Things to see in church

There may not be much to see that is different from usual. But look and see if you can see any of these:

the seats or any of the other furniture that has been moved

WELCOME TO ST. MARK'S

a small card to welcome newcomers

musicians with instruments

any extra things, like pictures and balloons

Colour in the pictures of the things you have seen.

About family services

In church there are services and groups for grown-ups and different groups for children and young people. But we are all one family in the church and so sometimes we do things all together.

At family services, people of all ages gather to worship God. There is something for everyone, whatever age you are.

A Bible verse for a family service

*Come, let us bow down and worship him;
let us kneel before the Lord, our Maker!
He is our God; we are the people he
cares for.*

Psalm 95:6–7a

What kinds of things do you do with others in your family? Do you go out together? Do you have a meal together? Do you play games, or go on holiday?

We do things together because we love each other and we enjoy being with each other.

We become members of the church family when we are baptized. We matter to God because he loves us all. We worship him together because we are all his family.

Thank you, Father God, for our church family. Bless us all as we worship you together. Amen

Something to do for a family service

Here is a church. Draw people of all ages going in for a family service. Or you could cut out pictures of people from a magazine and make a picture on this page.

A MOTHERING SUNDAY SERVICE

Things to see in church

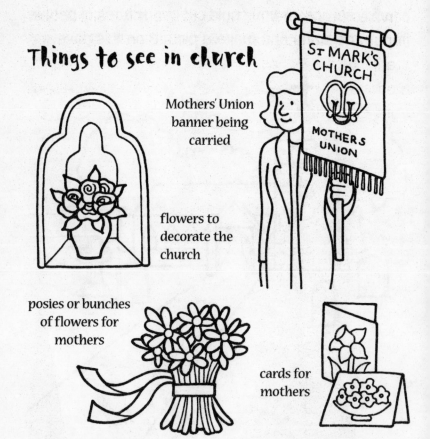

Mothers' Union banner being carried

ST MARK'S CHURCH

MOTHERS UNION

flowers to decorate the church

posies or bunches of flowers for mothers

cards for mothers

Colour in the pictures of the things you have seen.

About Mothering Sunday services

On a Sunday in the spring time, churches hold services for Mothering Sunday. We think about how important mothers are. We thank God for them and thank them for all that they do for us. Often, mothers are given flowers and a card as a present from the church.

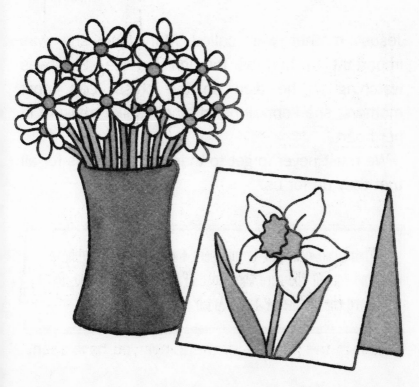

A Bible verse for a Mothering Sunday service

Jesus went back with his parents to Nazareth, where he was obedient to them. His mother treasured all these things in her heart.

Luke 2:51

Jesus' mother was called Mary and she was important to him all through his life. She was watching as he died on the cross. Like most mothers, she kept all her memories like treasure in her heart.

We must never forget to thank our mothers for all that they do for us.

> Thank you, dear God, for mothers, for all the love they have and for all the care they take of us. Thank you, too, for Mary the mother of Jesus. Amen

Something to do for a Mothering Sunday service

Make some of these cakes for your mother. Try to get another grown-up to help you so that they are a surprise for your mother.

You will need:
25g sugar,
25g butter,
25g cocoa,
1 tablespoon golden syrup,
25g cornflakes,
small paper cases.

1. Put the sugar, butter and cocoa into a pan.
2. Add the golden syrup.
3. Put the pan over the heat and melt the ingredients slowly, taking great care that they do not boil.
4. Add the cornflakes and stir them in with a wooden spoon.
5. When the cornflakes are thoroughly coated with the mixture, spoon into the cases and leave to set.

If you have enjoyed reading this book, look out for

My book of Special Times of year